This book ~~belongs to:~~
is shared with

_____

_____

_____

D1528539

the girl with waterfall eyes

to all who sparkle

© 2018 Conscious Stories LLC

Illustrations by Alexis Aronson

Published by
Conscious Stories LLC
1831 12th Avenue South, Ste 118
Nashville, TN, 37203

www.consciousstories.com

First Edition
Library of Congress
Control Number: 2018908432
ISBN 978-1-943-75014-6
JUV010000
JUVENILE FICTION / Bedtime & Dreams
JUV051000
JUVENILE FICTION / Imagination & Play
JUV046000
JUVENILE FICTION / Visionary &
Metaphysical

Printed in China

2 3 4 5 6 7 8 9 10

The last 20 minutes of every day are precious.

Dear parents, teachers, and readers,

This story has been gift-wrapped with two simple mindfulness practices
to help you connect more deeply with your children in the last 20
minutes of each day.

- Please set your intention for calm, open connection. Then start
  your story time with the **Snuggle Breathing Meditation**.
  Read each line aloud while taking slow deep breaths together.

- When we add loving eye contact to paired breathing, the
  connection between us grows, strengthening our feelings of
  safety and belonging.

- At the end of the story you will find **Kaleidoscope Eyes**.
  This will help you and your child connect by gazing at the
  amazing colors of each other's eyes, looking past the surface
  into each other's heart.

Enjoy Snuggling into Togetherness

Andrew

Snuggle Breathing

Let's begin our story by breathing together.
Say each line aloud and then
take a slow, deep breath in and out.

Breathing in, I breathe for me.

Breathing in, I breathe for you.

Breathing in, I breathe for us.

Breathing in, I breathe for all that surrounds us.

There was once a girl
who stood upon the world,
gazing at all of nature's beauty.

5

Waterfalls of light fell from her eyes,
trailing colors so beautiful.

Like a shower of petals
soft and gentle they fell,
bringing joy to all.

Moved by love,
she walked
with the rotation of the earth.

Each footstep landed
in perfect time and perfect place
to keep her balance
and the balance of the world.

Flowers of radiant colors grew
behind each step,
spreading her happiness
and marking her path
with love.

11

It was said that she could see
through storms and clouds,
beyond all difficulties
into a person's soul.

And to be seen by her
was the greatest gift
a soul could ever hope for.

For in her eyes,
where the waterfalls parted,
was the mirror of all the beauty
the world has ever seen,
shining in perfect reflection.

At night,
as darkness fell,
the East disappeared.
Then the North and South and West.

Soon the whole world was lost below her.

Scared that she would stand on
something precious,
she stopped walking.

19

But the earth kept turning.

She lost her balance
and fell off the world.

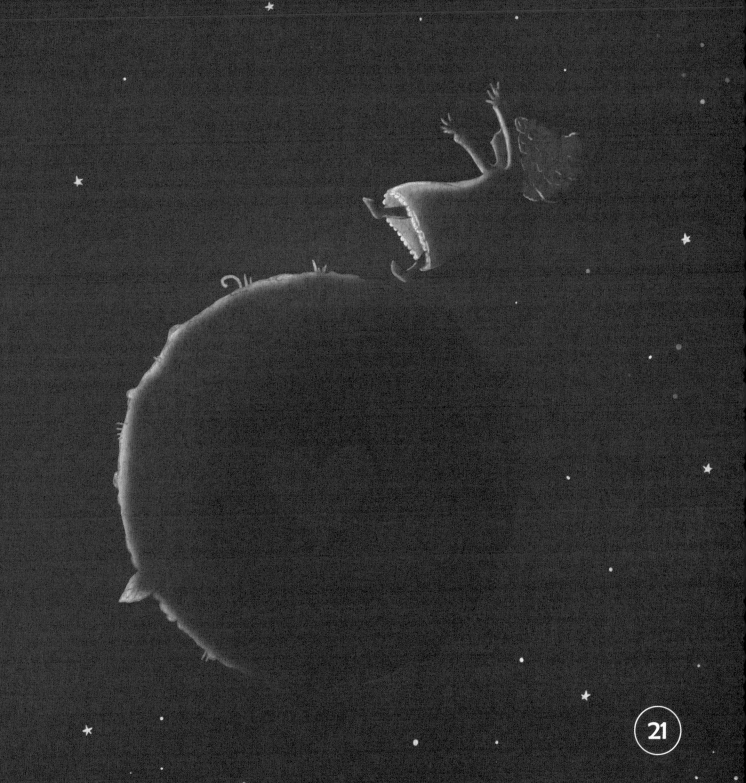

21

She drifted out into the darkness,
past the moon and past the stars.
Tumbling and twisting,
she fell through time and space,
past black holes and galaxies,
spiraling waterfall colors across the
dark night sky.

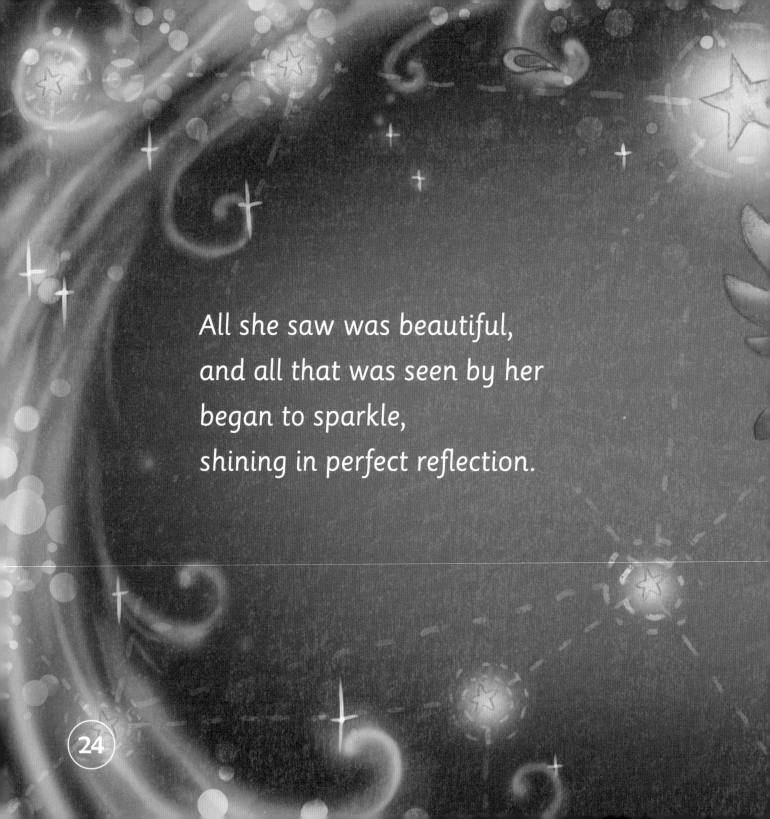

All she saw was beautiful,
and all that was seen by her
began to sparkle,
shining in perfect reflection.

25

As the sun's first rays dawned
across the universe,
every curve and spiral of her
nighttime waterfall twinkled
across the heavens,

making a clear path for her to
find her way ...

... home.

Eyes are the windows to the soul.

Have you seen the beauty of the world shining in another's Eyes?

Take a little time to grow connection and intimacy by meeting eye-to-eye before bedtime.

Gaze with love

Kaleidescope Eyes

1 Blink 3 times to begin.

2 Look into the eyes of your loved one.

3 Focus on the colors and patterns you see.

4 Now look deeper, beyond the surface, into each other's heart.

5 Breathe and smile.

6 Blink 3 times and close your eyes to complete.

Andrew Newman – author

Andrew Newman is the award-winning author and founder of www.ConsciousStories.com, a growing series of bedtime stories purpose-built to support parent-child connection in the last 20 minutes of the day. His professional background includes deep training in therapeutic healing work and mindfulness. He brings a calm yet playful energy to speaking events and workshops, inviting and encouraging the creativity of his audiences, children K-5, parents, and teachers alike.

Alexis Aronson – illustrator

Alexis is a self-taught illustrator, designer and artist from Cape Town, South Africa. She has a passion for serving projects with a visionary twist that incorporates image making with the growth of human consciousness for broader impact. Her media ranges from digital illustration and design to fine art techniques, such as intaglio printmaking, ceramic sculpture, and painting. In between working for clients and creating her own art for exhibition, Alexis is an avid nature lover, swimmer, yogi, hiker, and gardener.

www.alexisaronson.com

Follow Conscious Bedtime Stories on Facebook / Instagram / Twitter

I see you

I see you

I see you

I see you

I see you

I see you

I see you

I see you

I see you

I see you

I see you

I see you

The Conscious Bedtime Story Club

snuggling into togetherness

**stickers
for
sharing**

and for your
Star Counter

Star Counter

Every time you breathe together and read aloud, you make a star shine in the night sky.

Place a sticker, or color in a star, to count how many times you have read this book.